Birds of the Air

Birds of the Air

DAVID YEZZI

CARNEGIE MELLON UNIVERSITY PRESS
PITTSBURGH 2013

ACKNOWLEDGMENTS

Grateful acknowledgment is made to the editors of the following publications, where poems in this book, sometimes in different forms, first appeared: *The Atlantic*, *Columbia Magazine*, *Edinburgh Review*, *First Things*, *Linebreak*, *New England Review*, *New Ohio Review*, *The New York Times*, *PN Review*, *Smartish Pace*, *Smithsonian*, *Think Journal*, *TriQuarterly*, and *Verse Daily*.

"Cough," "Crane," "Flatirons," "Itchy," and "Lazy," first appeared in *Poetry*.

"Minding Rites" appeared in *The Best American Poetry 2012*, edited by Mark Doty and David Lehman.

"Free Period" was included in *Poetry Speaks: Who I Am*, edited by Elise Paschen and Dominique Raccah, and in *The Swallow Anthology of New American Poets*.

Dirty Dan & Other Travesties (including "Dirty Dan," "Spoils," and "Tomorrow & Tomorrow") was performed at the Bowery Poetry Club in March 2010. Produced by Verse Theater Manhattan and directed by Richard Ryan, it featured music by Chris Lee and performances by Bruce Faulk, Chris Lee, Sayra Player, Tony Torn, Max Woertendyke, and David Yezzi.

"Birds of the Air" was printed in a fine-press single-fold edition by Aralia Press (2011).

"Tomorrow & Tomorrow" appeared as a limited-edition chapbook from Exot Books (2012), with an afterword by Denis Donoghue.

"Flatirons" was printed in a fine-press edition, along with Ernest Hilbert's "Glacier," as *Two Ranges* by Nemean Lion Press (2012).

Designed by Sara-Anne Lee

Library of Congress Control Number 2012949881
ISBN: 978-0-88748-571-8

10 9 8 7 6 5 4 3 2 1

CONTENTS

for Sarah

And what will you do now? How will you live?

As birds do, mother.

I

CRANE

Paper creased is
with a touch
made less by half,
reduced as much

again by a second
fold — so the wish
to press our designs
can diminish

what we hold.
But by your hand's
careful work,
I understand

how this unleaving
makes of what's before
something finer
and finally more.

LAZY

I don't say things I don't want to say
or chew the fat with fat cats just because.

With favor-givers who want favors back,
I tend to pass on going for the ask.

I send, instead, a series of regrets,
slip the winding snares that people lay.

The unruffledness I feel as a result,
the lank repose, the psychic field of rye

swayed in wavy air, is my respite
among the shivaree of clanging egos

on the packed commuter train again tonight.
Sapping and demeaning—it takes a lot

to get from bed to work and back to bed.
I barely go an hour before I'm caught

wincing at the way that woman laughs
or he keeps clucking at his magazine.

And my annoyance fills me with annoyance.
It's laziness that lets them seem unreal

—a radio with in-and-out reception
blaring like hell when it finally hits a station.

The song that's on is not the one I'd hoped for,
so I wait distractedly for what comes next.

BIRDS OF THE AIR

She's the trunk and they're the blowing branches:
the seagulls mass around her as she scatters
bread crusts grabbed from a plastic grocery bag.
They dip to her, since bread is all that matters.

She casts the crumbs in lamplight, over water,
to gulls who catch her manna on the wing—
snatching their staple needs straight from the air,
the sky replete with every wanted thing,

until it seems that they might live off giving.
Back in the bag, her right hand burrows in
and finds a further hunk of loaf and chucks it
into the glinting sleet. The cries begin,

and, without fail, bread finds another mouth.
After she goes, the dark birds settle back.
They float south with the floes along the bank,
their fortune pitched in wind, the water black.

SPOILS

Money I've made lots of different ways:
back-to-back shifts at the Cumberland Farms,
downing burritos out of the microwave,
late-night entertainment being a wall
of glossy mags behind the register
in racks below the cigarettes and scratchers —
all that honey-colored flesh air-brushed to perfection,
pristine among the milk crates and the soot.
Or: in gleaming dayrooms of the nursing home,
where I would mop up urine underneath
the wheelchairs of the jittering demented,
who were oblivious, it seemed to me,
to the television they were pointed at.
Lunch hours in the trailer in the lot,
with this sweet misfit kid — my boss — and his
boss, discussing daily what they'd do
if they won the Lottery: retire to Boca.
Buy a Caddy. No, a Lexus.
                    So, one day,
out by the nurses' station, there's these two
patients side by side in wheelchairs,
waiting for the nurse to take them back
to their rooms, or maybe down to therapy,
when this old guy, Edward was his name —
Edward, he was famous for this shit.
Edward's sitting there next to this lady,
Ethel, I think her name was. Can't remember.
At any rate, so I'll just call her Ethel
for the purpose of the story, or this part
of it, the point of which I want to come to
now, and that is this: Ethel, right?
Ethel's got this great enormous smile

on her face, like Thomas Merton or the Buddha.
Her gums stretch from her forehead to her chin,
all molars and gold fillings, and her head
is swaying back and forth in fits, like nodding,
because Edward (you gotta love this guy)
has got his hand way up under her skirt.
And though she only half knows that he's there
she's loving it, just loving it. Old Ethel.
Until the nurses come and separate
the two, and send him packing, full of scolds,
with Edward donkey-laughing, very pleased,
the bad boy of the dayroom and God bless him.
He wasn't the only one.
All the nuts were there: the guy who yelled
"Ay," but long and loud, like *Aaaaayyyyyyyyy.*
Aaaaaaaayyyyyy. Aaaaaaayyyyyyyyy.
All day we'd hear him, from the parking lot.
Or the dude with elephantiasis they called Plato,
or the woman turned a hundred who would ask,
"Are you my mother? Are you my mother?"

        And occasionally a bed
would just go empty, overnight, like that.
And one of the regular crew was gone—
to the hospital—and just as often as not
that would be it; they wouldn't come back.
Their photos would come down, the woolen throw
would disappear, the tchotchkes, crosses, slippers,
packed up by a nurse, or family.
Thrown away, mostly. It's amazing how
most of the stuff we live with, cherish, hoard

is so utterly worthless when we're gone,
turned instantly to trash.
                              That's another job
I had. Not regularly, just once or twice.
Clean up after people who had died.
The first time was somewhere out on Long Island.
I was just a year or two out of college,
cold calling for cosmetics companies
in a high-rise on the East Side, six to ten.
So I was glad to get the cash and all the books
I could carry: the guy was a professor,
or a rabbi — Schopenhauer, Aristotle's
Ethics. I still have them somewhere here.

But the time I'm really talking about was when
I stole a gold watch from a dying man.
Right?
                 His apartment was . . . well, unbelievable.
Peering from the hallway door, it looked
like the inside of a trash compactor.

I was shown in by a man I'd never met.
He knew the man whose place it was: a neighbor.
We'll say this neighbor's name is Mr. V.
His friend was sick, said V., a nursing home.
He wasn't coming back to this apartment,
not dead, you see, but never coming back.
My job was to sort out all of the trash,
which was everywhere, on every surface,
like the very air had sprouted clods of mold,
smelly tumors. Everywhere. More trash.
Clogging up the closets, in the kitchen,

bathroom cabinets, dresser, sofa, sink.
Mostly, it was papers, tiny papers.
He never threw away a single shred.
ATM receipts and old prescriptions —
brown paper grocery bags stuffed full of them.
And I sat there for hours cramming armloads
of this crap into giant Hefty bags,
big ones, like the ones you use for lawns.
I went through every shoebox, every carton,
sorting every piece before I chucked it.
Why? Because I *had* to sort them all.
Because every now and then I'd find a photo
or a postcard or a letter to this guy,
who had been sick six years, the neighbor said.
So that's why so much stuff: the piles of garbage,
the takeout bags from food he'd had delivered.
Tucked in with all this junk was this guy's life:
Kodaks of him getting off a plane
in the bright Israeli sunshine, with his suit
and dark glasses, his thin tie and the shadow
of his fedora, his smile at being home.
Postcards from someone he loved in Florida.
He ran a successful business, apparently,
jewelry and importing, said Mr. V.
In the closet was a collection of wrist watches,
dozens of them, boxes of old watches,
in every style, for men and women, modern
and antique, both.
                    The one I took was gold,
from the closet where I'd been lying on my belly
for nearly half an hour, excavating
bags of stockpiled clothing. On the floor,

I found these vintage watches with no straps,
and when I knew that old V. wasn't watching,
I stuck two in my pocket. (Two I took,
I remember that now.)
                              As I was leaving,
the neighbor says to me, "You're a good boy.
Take a watch. Go on and pick one out."
I say, "No, I don't usually wear a watch.
No, really, thanks. I really couldn't use one."
The air outside was cold, near Christmastime,
like tonight. And I walked north on Upper Broadway,
to a jewelry store and stopped and bought a band.

What was that, like fifteen years ago?
I've only got the one now.
It doesn't keep good time, and I can't afford
to have it cleaned. I've worn it only once
or twice. To make an impression. So I keep it
in a box inside my closet, and though I haven't
had it out in years I know it's there.
What were they going to do, sell it,
and use the money for the nursing home?
I thought a lot about that, afterwards.
Did he need the money to keep him in that place?
I doubt it, you know. Medicaid, Medicare,
whatever the fuck.
                              It kind of haunts me though,
a little, if you want to know. You know?
I can't ever bring myself to throw it out.
Whenever something bad happens to me,
I think of that watch. Like when you died
so young that way. I know I made it worse—

not being around enough, keeping away
as much as I could till it was too late,
and you'd gone.
                    So, what's the secret of the watch?
A man was dying, and I took his watch.
It was his, and then it wasn't; it was trash.
And now that it is mine, I keep it safe,
until it's time for someone else to clean out
my closet, and, whoever's job it is,
he makes off with it or he passes it on
or most likely of all
just drops it into a bag and throws it out.

ITCHY

Hard to reach, so you yank your clothes
getting at it—the button at your neck,
the knotted shoe. You snake your fingers in
until your nails possess the patch of skin
that's eating you. And now you're in the throes
of ecstasy, eyes lolling in your skull,
as if sensing the first time the joy one takes
in being purely animal.

It's so good to have a scratch,
though isn't it a drag living like this,
jounced on a high wire of impulses,
every wish the same programmed response
to another signal passed from cell to cell,
amounting in the end to a distraction—
if truth be told—from rarer things, thoughts free
from the anchor-chain of self?

For even the least sweetness, we
behave like the old man on the low wall
I saw outside the hospital today,
who had his hand inside his flannel shirt,
scratching at his chest, trancelike, agog,
his eyelids fluttering like butterflies
in a meadow of snowy Queen Ann's lace.
I never saw him stop.

Such root satisfaction is like
the dying desert legionnaire's in films,
when he finds, against all odds, a water jug
and, lifting it, delights to feel it heavy.
The score swells, his eyes relume. He yanks

the stopper out, then fills his mouth with sand.
Though, worse: we've seen the film; we know it's sand;
we gulp it anyway.

COUGH

I see you once I've got you down to size:
a two-day-stubble squatter; jailbait eyes;

the bottle-headed trophy mom; the mentor
always angling his face down from the center

of his universe to shine a light on yours.
The fated anorexic, whose allures

shimmer in the mirror for her eyes
only, denying what her denial denies.

Once you become a cliché I can hate you —
or, treat me tenderly and let me date you.

But that only retards the writing-off
that comes with boredom, amour propre, or (*cough*)

irreconcilable differences, i.e.,
those things about you that are least like me,

yet just slightly different, my foible's homophone,
so in hating yours I really hate my own.

This keeps the focus where it ought to be —
On whom, you ask? Invariably on. . . . See?

I didn't even have to say it, did I?
I love you so much. No need to reply.

II

FREE PERIOD

Outside study hall,
it's me, my girlfriend, and a guy
named Rob—bony kid, klutzy
at games, fluent in French.
    He's behind her;

I'm asleep or half-
asleep (it's morning), and, as I
squint into the trapezoid of light
breaking on the bench and me,
    I see him raise

his hand to her head
from the back, so gently
she doesn't notice
him at first, but stands there,
    carved in ebony

and beaten gold:
Stacey's straight black hair
falling in shafts of sun.
He smoothes it down,
    firmly now,

so that she turns,
kind of freaked, as if to say,
"Can you believe it?"
to me still coming to.
    Yes, I guess I can,

I think to myself,
with only a twinge
of jealousy, with admiration,
actually. And pity—since he'd seen
beauty raw,

for which humiliation
was the smallest price,
and, dazzled, grasped at it,
not getting hold.
It wasn't his, god knows,

or mine, as I,
months later, learned
hopelessly—almost fatally,
it felt—or even hers, though it was
of her and around her,

in that freeze-frame
of low sunshine,
with us irremediably young
and strung-out from love
and lack of love.

FLATIRONS

i.

From the false summit, coxcomb-cum-arête,
cool thermals underscore our frailties,
past edges where our wingless feet are set
and the long look down dilutes the evergreens.
As sandstone ends, the world of ghosts begins—
they sometimes rise up still in dreams, my love.
With one hand firm, I step onto the skin
of the abyss, embracing what's above
and severing spent ties to the scree below.
The filtered light turns lichen eerie green,
ushering in a world we hardly know,
at least not one we're sure we've ever seen
just so, each climber brand new in his skin,
no longer mired in waiting to begin.

ii.

The whisper clings beside you as you rise
along the ice melt, following the chalk.
Its cadence is the thrum behind your eyes;
your trembling, the music of its talk.
No longer trust your arms; they're paid with fear.
Along the rock, the grip that's hidden there,
invisible but sure, will not appear
until you trade your fast-hold for the air,
and, as you reach, it ripples like a pool
in which your newfound safety now reflects:
the diastole of breath becomes the rule
for governing what atmosphere elects—
to claim this height as owed to us in spirit,
although we risk ourselves to answer it.

iii.

Free solo: dearest, I am losing you,
not now (one hopes!) but slowly, over time.
Admit that there is nothing left to do
but re-devote our efforts to the climb,
remembering that the second side is less
than a reprieve—more sheer and far from kind—
before the gentle, sloping wilderness
enwraps us and we let go of the sky.
Your living hand guides home my dangled foot.
At gravity's unlikely slant, we smear
across the arkose, knowing that the root
has taken hold deep in the layers. Here,
a thrust-fault pushed up rock, and, as it rose,
it found its altitude in its repose.

iv.

Pinned to the face, you close the aperture —
no way looks right, and there is no way down
but keeping on — returning's hot allure
hissing its false promises, the sound
of the last support beam loudly giving way.
What is it that wipes the rock free of direction?
The crystal ceiling that began the day
goes black, almost it seems without detection.
The open door blows shut; the empty glass
brims over and, when raised, is dry again:
time's bait-and-switch. An hour from the pass,
wind drags high clouds across the peak; just then
the air grows cold. Our backs turn to the weather,
as a way comes clear, ascending with no tether.

v.

It's when we're most engaged with other things
that the angel enters, a twist in temperature,
a lightness in the chest that we call wings.
Giddy with sacrament and the impure
gluttony of blood and air and skin,
we look with panoramic eyes to where
the earth curls under and the sky begins,
though we ourselves are of this light-shot air,
senses extending without obstacle,
reaching past by rooting down though rock —
obdurate kindness, heaven's window sill.
We are as useless as an open lock,
more insubstantial than a drinking song,
and marked by sandstone long after we're gone.

DIZZY

Zigging, mid-
block, he's off:
on a torn-up, trafficked slab of Second Avenue—
his cane sweeping
over

broken asphalt,
like a sapper or
an open skiff on back-splashing seas. For a few
seconds it's
unclear

if he gets
the risk,
as yellow cabs swoop down and flock at the light.
Then, safe
home

on the other
side. And I
for one cannot take my eyes off him as he pivots,
compassing
north.

We're never
truly clear.
Now he jams himself at pace between a giant planter
and cross-braced
scaffold

newly set up
at Finnegans.
And *wham*. The guy is smack on his ass, un-staring up
to heaven,
stunned.

Damn,
I think, what
in hell was that? It's not like the pain of loving someone
who doesn't
want

you back
(though that
once ate up years of my life and left me blown like an artery
after too many
bypasses),

nor does it
compare to
frittering away in a job that I'm ill-suited to and which I'll
probably
lose.

It's more
as if a hammer
dropped from a sill and laid him out cold. That scaffold
just appeared there
overnight.

And for all
my hard-won bile
I'm not worse off than he is, except in this: I've come
to think I
am.

DIRTY DAN

I can't remember what the night was like.
It was, *phssh*, twenty-. . . seven? years ago,
before I even knew you. I was home,
from college maybe, hanging out with friends?
Christmas break, it must have been. And cold.
Too bad you never saw him. Too late now,
not just because there's no way Dirty Dan
is still alive (he was ancient, even then),
but more because you are not, so prematurely . . .

So: Dan. I only saw him once. Just once.
I guess that's part of it. It snowed that night.
(Let's pretend that we're both sitting around
in your living room, just telling stories.)
Now, it's my turn, right? So—Dirty Dan.
I swear to god this guy was unbelievable:
this wiry geezer, bug-eyed, in a toque,
white short-sleeve chef shirt and a stubble beard.
But wait, hold on, back up. So, this is Dan:
a short-order cook with ice blue, staring eyes . . .
I need to tell you a bit about before.
At any rate, it's late one night, and I'm
home from school on break. I'm seeing friends
and drunk and underage and talking "art"
with Julie and her boyfriend Mitch, who's just
like a miniature professor with bad skin.
He's smart and tweedy and totally insane
and also so completely full of shit,
which I like. And mostly he likes books
and getting stoned and talking late. Talk, talk.
And then, long-suffering Julie, small and preppy,
and really very cute, I think sometimes.

One minute, Mitch is spouting Joyce—about
how all he actually wanted was to write
a really good read crammed with lots of jokes
for all his friends to savor, to make them laugh.
Next: the neon blur and flat pink light
of a diner by the park.
                                    I remember this:
the snow and cold and Mitch rubbing his hands
together, as he says, "Let's go see Dan,"
then we're in a booth.
                                    The place is packed.
It's 3 a.m., and there must be a dozen
booths like ours. The counter's jammed with kids
who've come from Luna, dancing, high and freeze-framed
in strobe flashes and ethereal black light.
And now they're beat and hungry, after-hours,
giving up their orders to these guys,
also kids, who write down all the coffee
and toast and juice and ham and bacon sides,
the eggs—fried, scrambled, over easy, up—
and call them out across the room to Dan.
Our voices mingle in the greasy air,
talking bullshit, screaming with delight,
goofing, over which the waiters' voices
fly like homing birds,
                                    while, at the grill,
Dan shuttles like a Chinese acrobat,
balancing every order in his mind
like so many plates spun on wooden dowels,
never dropping one, and grunting out
he'd got the order, pick up twenty-one.
And we were there to watch. And snarl-haired Mitch,

who, I just remembered, lost a tooth,
or, no, he had a denture he'd remove
that left this gaping hole each time he'd laugh.
We laughed all night that night.
                                    That's why we got
together in the first place, why we drank
and smoked and talked of books. That's why we went
to see Dan in his kitchen, to be amazed,
the way that the whole diner was amazed,
the way the kids who took the orders were amazed.
Dirty Dan was this incredible
freaking genius. Brilliant. You think it's easy?
Try it. What he did was just not something
anyone can do; he knew it, too.
You could tell. How he would yell in a rage
when two of the kid waiters talked at once,
screwing up his groove — and they'd apologize,
since the last thing they wanted to do was break
his perfect streak that ran till 5 a.m.
It was like riding down the trough of a wave
that started somewhere out in the Pacific.
God, how we roared. That's all we really wanted
was to laugh.
                        And you were like that, too, I guess.
That's the way it always went, wasn't it?
Open the wine, talk books, reel off new jokes
that always had some place inside the flow
of a larger conversation for the night,
and a place, too, in breaking the tick, tick,
of dingy sink, cold coffee, quiet phone,
afternoon nap, and too much television,
which haunted you in daylight till the night

came back and, ranting, after-hours, we'd people
the vastness with our stories and we'd laugh.

Now you're dead, I wonder more and more
whom I should tell them to, stories like this,
running through them in my head mostly.
Julie and Mitch? *Pfft.* I can't really say
what happened to them. Did they ever marry?
I doubt it.
Julie must have had more sense than that.
Don't get me wrong; Mitch was my friend, too.
(He was the one who called him Dirty Dan,
cackling and growling with his gap-tooth grin.)
We were a lot alike.
Now I don't know where they are. Alive?
Somewhere? Nowhere?
                              Too long ago to know. I laugh
a lot less with them gone. Does that surprise you?

for Tom Disch

MINDING RITES

This guy I know, a rabbi, Friday nights,
on his way home before sunset in winter,
always stops at a florist or bodega
and buys a bunch of flowers for his wife.

Every week the same, a ritual,
regardless of her mood that morning, fresh
upsets at work, or snarling on the bridge;
he brings her roses wrapped in cellophane.

But isn't there a ring of hokiness
in that? Why should a good man have to show
his devotion? Some things go unspoken;
some things get tested on the real world,

and isn't that the place that matters most?
So when you told me I should bring you flowers,
I joked, "But don't I show my feelings more
in dog walks, diapers, and rewiring lamps?"

The flowers, I learned later, weren't for wooing,
not for affection in long marriage, but
for something seeded even deeper down,
through frost heaves, and which might be, roughly, peace.

(It's funny that I just assumed romance.)
Now there's no peace with us, I wonder what
they might have meant to you, those simple tokens,
holding in sight what no rite can grow back.

ORTS

Tough to say from this tableful of scraps
what couples featsed here—gnawed olive stones
among the burnt ends of cold meat, the laps
of cantaloupes splayed open, spindly bones
of game birds, unloaved crusts, a waxy rind.
Did late-harvest wine unloose their wild talk?
Whose restless eyes, at once far-off and kind,
looked skyward on an after-dinner walk?
The clues are hard to tease out: were they fair
or compromised; temperate or gluttonous;
did some not give a fig and others care?
Both, perhaps, and in both just like us,
who, swept up in the whirl of tonight's laughter,
pay no special mind to what comes after.

PALS

They don't shy from the give-and-take:
the more you deke, the more they're jake.

The more you fume, the tougher they back you,
denouncing non-pals who attack you.

They are your mirror's best reflection.
They'll knock on doors for your election.

And pals pay back. No pal's too pure
to find his pal a sinecure.

If you have doubts, pals will ease them;
if guilty thoughts, let pals appease them.

A pal can lead you to the trough
or help you take a few pounds off

with just a word—it's common fact—
and, failing that, they manage tact.

It's for the best. That's all pals wish you.
They take your side on every issue.

Pals find means to fit your ends,
but how long they stay pals depends

on the ways you are simpatico.
How do they know? Pals know. They know.

III

TOMORROW & TOMORROW

a travesty

I

"What's done cannot be undone."

Am I right?

So . . . obvious. So irrefutable.
Of course, if it is done it can't be undone.
Any idiot knows that. Or else:
"If it were done, when 'tis done, then 'twere well
it were done quickly."

"When the hurly-burly's done."

"Is execution done on Cawdor?"
"Yet let that be
Which the eye fears, when it is done, to see."
You see? Stuff happens, you can't take it back.
Just one of those things you don't have to say,
but sometimes we still need reminding of:
"What's done is done." So good, it's like a spell,
a charm, a bell: *done, done.* But Lady Macbeth?
She wasn't the only one who said it; no,
others said it. Sophocles, for instance,
he said it, something like it; said it long
before her, if you want to know the truth.
Lots of people said it, and it's true.

I did that play, a million years ago.   .
And every night I'd listen from the wings
and hear those lines.

I was an actor. Sort of.

Or, technically, more like a waiter. So,
I'd pick up part-time shifts behind the bar,
serving Mai Tais underneath the whale
at the American Museum of Natural History—

revolving-door jobs in the service industry
broken up by brief forays on stage.
Here's a couple more, in case you missed it:
"In every point twice done and then done double."
"I have done no harm."
                    (That's what they always say.)

The show was a disaster. Every night,
we died a dozen deaths on different stages.
Macbeth and Lady, they were really married,
married in real life, and they produced it.
In Germany — in English but in Germany.
In western Germany before the wall
came down.
                    The other waiters were so excited
when they heard I got a job, that I was Malcolm,
they bought me drinks and gave me this old book:
a beat-up phrase book unearthed at the Strand,
Berlitz or something, and completely worthless.
It must have been from fifty years ago.
Oh, and it had lots of useful stuff,
like "Es tut mir leid, ich habe meinen Teller zebrochen,"
which means, I think, "I'm sorry, I've broken my plate,"
or other things that I probably would need
like "Ist es Zeit für meine Spritze?":
"Is it time for my injection?"
I remember looking over at my girlfriend
just then — Sasha, a dancer. That made her laugh.
Her teeth were too big and a bit off-center
in a way that made me always want to kiss her.
                    "I go, and it is done;
the bell invites me."

Before we left, we froze our asses off:
rehearsing in some empty public school
on 6th and B — no heat and no hot water,
when people slept in tents in Tompkins Square.
Kids would throw M-80s off the roofs —
these huge explosions — and we'd have to run for it.
We'd step outside to smoke a cigarette,
and they'd come streaming down like, *holy shit!*
By dark, the place cleared out:
syringes in the walkups, random gun-pops,
vials strewn in doorways like bright glass
from a car wreck.
                                    So, I told my waiting job
so long and stuffed a backpack full of clothes.
I can't remember what we said that morning,
Sasha and I. There's lot's I don't remember.
Though some of it's still there, a skin, invisible.
Some things you never quite recover from.
I left. So what was I supposed to do?

                                    You know the curse?
You're not supposed to say the word *Macbeth;*
instead you say the "Scottish Tragedy,"
which sounds ridiculous, but there you have it.
Let's say we're talking in the dressing room,
and I say the name Macbeth, you know, accidentally.
Actors have this thing, they have this code
(or not a code; it's more of a behavior):
I'm supposed go outside and close the door,
I turn around three times, say *shit* or *fuck!*,
and then I knock and ask to come back in.

It's kind of cool, 'cause then it's like a safety,
like canceling something bad: you take it back.
But cursed? Do people ever think they are?
Who thinks they're cursed? You think, we'll that's not good,
or that's a string of bad luck, a bad year,
but no one thinks they're cursed. Not at the time.

The play was bad, no doubt.
                            It wasn't that.
Some things just sort of happened. Little things
at first, annoying stuff, like props gone missing.
But then we crashed the van: Lady Macbeth
was driving. She spun out on the Autobahn
and had to do the tour in a cast—
"Out damned spot . . ." She'd start rubbing the plaster,
night after night, sleepwalking, in a trance.
And after that I did begin to think
that maybe we were cursed. It felt like that,
like we'd done something wrong.
                         It tells you things
that you don't want to know—about yourself,
about how you think everything is fine,
then one cold morning with the snow outside
you wake up sweating from an awful dream,
convinced that you have done things so unspeakable . . .
What if you did, only you didn't know it?
Or, more likely, knew it, then forgot.
Something you'd never believe in a thousand years:
murder your father, sleep with your own mother,
those kind of things.
But that's a different play.

II

This is the way the line's supposed to go.
The battle's over, right? We won: our side.
And Banquo spends the night in Macbeth's castle.
When he gets there, he looks up and sees this swift
nesting in the rafters there. This scarred
old warrior, this patriarch of kings
is so moved by the sight of this, he makes
a joke about the song birds having sex.
He sniffs the air and says:

> *This guest of summer,*
> *The temple-haunting martlet, does approve,*
> *By his loved mansionry, that the heaven's breath*
> *Smells wooingly here; no jutty, frieze,*
> *Buttress, nor coign of vantage, but this bird*
> *Hath made his pendent bed and procreant cradle.*
> *Where they most breed and haunt, I have observ'd*
> *The air is delicate.*

Something like that.
So, our guy comes.

Our Banquo's name is Bill,
and Bill's this graying hippy from the Village,
who pays a dollar-fifty rent, he says,
which frees him up to do a bit of acting.
So, Bill comes out; he looks up in the grid,
with three or four of us just standing there,
and Duncan, who's the king, so hugely fat
he's like a minivan. So, Bill looks up.
(He's downstage.) He looks down. He looks at us:
"This . . . bird," he says.

And he's completely up:

that's when you're off the script, you're up, you're *up*.
You've no idea who you are or what
you're doing.
                    It's, I guess, a bit like drowning,
like being under water, but too deep.
You go into a kind of panic mode —
the world slows down and hangs there at a distance.
From the cold murky bottom you look up
and see the small disk of the sun receding,
and you realize you haven't got the air
to get back up. So you begin to swim,
then lose your bearings in a cloud of bubbles.
King Duncan sees this — Duncan's name is Neil —
Duncan sees that Bill's completely jammed,
so what he does is . . . throw the guy a bone?
Skip ahead and pick up later on?
No, no. He stands there, doesn't say a word,
steps forward even, sort of cranes his neck,
as if to say, "Uh-huh? We're list-en-ing."
I tell you, actors — they're a pack of dogs,
completely warped.
                    Still, it was all good fun.
Lady's in a cast, the show's a bomb.
Not even knowing German, we could tell
the papers thought we were a total joke.
But we were getting paid and seeing sights
and drinking beer. A lot.

I can't forget that show, and not because
I was freest then or wildest or whatever,
Just, parts of it keep coming back that way.
Or, earlier:

It's snowing. We're on Jane Street,
with wood smoke rising from the townhouses.
Sasha's in lace-up boots and woolen tights,
short skirt from which her dancer's legs
are shooshing in the cold.
She's pouting over something, and I'm hanging
on every word and sigh, on every turn
of her moods, and there were many, same as me.
Across the avenue, up sagging steps
to a tiny place she shared with another girl.
The roommate hated me, 'cause every night
we'd show up late then quickly disappear
into the bedroom — closet, crawl space, lair,
barely big enough to squeeze a mattress in —
and close the door and make love with the lights on.
I would call her name out like a chant,
repeating it with every exhalation,
soft in her ear at first, then loud, then louder,
as we fell backward over a high wall
into blankness.
                              It's stuff like that stays with you.
So when her voice came to me over the line
in a phone booth in Cologne, near the cathedral,
the gist of it was like the crack of ice
constricting on a mountainside, and I
realized if I hung up the phone
that would be it.

There's someone outside waiting for the booth.
After five minutes in the ice and snow,
he starts banging on the door as if to say
when will you be done, I need the phone.

And I'm behind the glass, just hanging on,
and asking her how come she's back with him.
He's in the room. I think I almost hear him.
I know because she talked to him that way.
He'd call when I was there, and she'd pretend
I wasn't, which was cruel of her and sexy.
He's right there, and she's naked, on the edge
of the futon, and it's nine o'clock in the morning.
And now the German guy starts hammering
his fist against the booth, so I just stop.

It's funny: I remember bits and pieces:
the caramel-colored duvet and the curl
her lip made when she smiled, her body leaning
above me, choking laughter hoarse with tears,
the way her eyes were like a little kid's.
I thought, that's it, you know?

                               I started reading
the Bible. I tore out the Old Testament
and carried it around. But you don't die.
You live for longer than you think you will.
Of course, there's things that won't let you forget
how what you wanted is what hurt you most,
how it was happiness itself betrayed you.

"Well, let's away and say how much is done."

III

Snow was piling up knee-deep in Munich,
at least where we were staying in the cramped
side streets near the station — a Turkish slum.
And we were in a war.
             "Kein Blut für Öl"
was scrawled in red spray paint across the walls.
They didn't want us there. Nobody did.

             "We are all Germans here,"
some radish-faced Bayerische drunkard yells
over the Beatles in the Café Americain —
that's right, the damned Café *Americain*.
He yells it at Macduff, an Irish guy,
(not Scots, but close enough for bus and truck).
We got a lot of that, both north and south.
So, here's the Black Forest. Here's the North Sea.
Let's say this squiggly line's the Autobahn,
and every day we'd drive at record speed
from Aachen to Stuttgart, Stuttgart to Freiberg,
Freiberg to Cologne, four towns a week.

Because I'm Malcolm, I get to be the king,
which I thought was pretty cool, except, get this,
my grand finale always got a laugh.
I'm up there pouring out my guts, and just
as I start to raise the crown above my head
(a moment that you dream about in school)
with stage light pouring through this golden O
— that's when the laughter starts.
             And not just giggles.

No, no. A nervous laugh, like wildfire.
It wasn't just my acting, though that was bad
enough — more lame than laughable, I'm sure.
They laughed because each night, right at the curtain,
they'd fly in a giant banner of my head
to replace the one they'd torn down of Macbeth.
The drops were painted by some kid in Queens,
with tempera paint or house paint, I don't know.
So, when they dropped the thing, each night we'd hear
this far-off rumble like an engine grinding.
This floor-to-ceiling banner of my face
was fucking cross-eyed. You believe that shit?

Did you ever see Polanski's film *Macbeth?*
It's got great stuff. But mostly that's because
Kenneth Tynan told him what was what.
Banquo's children shall be kings, we know.
We also know that Malcolm's on the throne.
So, here's the thing.
Macbeth has got no kids, or none we know of.
But Lady's given suck, that's how she puts it,
so what is that? What happened to her kid?
(I know, I'm getting literal.) Behind the credits,
a figure in a cloak — who must be Banquo's son —
goes to see the witches. It never ends.
One thane betrays another, blood for blood,
Blood against blood. And so on and on.
Sometimes it's hard to know how it began,
how what they wanted was the thing they wanted.
"What's to be done?"

                    Days off we used for sightseeing:
end of the streetcar line, there is the fence,

then squares marking the places that they slept.
Behind is the iron door that kept the flames,
and overhead the sky where they saw the smoke.

The gate on which we read the words was here.
Behind the gate, the path bends to the left.
The crematorium is sort of here.

Half of us could easily have died there.
Half of us would have been the ones who lived.

IV

I don't want to talk about it. Only . . .
change the subject, can we? Twenty years,
so long I can't remember who I was.
Though mostly I'm the same. I have the same
marks set down against me on the slate.
That's how I think of it sometimes, like marks,
like hash marks on a perfect field of white.

The sun is setting in you, the snow is falling in you . . .

I hate this song. It's crap.
                              And mostly I
Don't think about it, really. Why do that?
I only get more miserable that way.
We'd talk at night. He'd call from Germany.
He was in a play. So, yeah, we'd talk.
Which was the worst, since months went by
that I couldn't tell him. I just couldn't.

Your face is like a mirror, your face inside my mirror . . .

I prayed, you know, that it might not be true:
the lateness. Then I'm ten or twelve weeks on,
and he's off god-knows-where, calling me up
on Sunday mornings. I think I kind of lost it.
Enough, I thought, enough, you know? I told him
I was back with my old boyfriend. That was it.
He never called me after that. Which scared me.

How can it be the same, if it was never that way?

It was just simpler on my own, and I
didn't want to know what he would say . . .
didn't want to see him give that look
like I should know exactly what to do.
I had no help, and I did what I did,
the only thing that at the time made sense.
A life ago. That's not me anymore.

It's just the tide of your eyes, washing away the shore.

You can hear church bells from here. If you
wait a minute we can hear them now.
The bells are like the snow. They make things quiet.
And when they ring then everything around them
is quiet and the sound of quiet is
the sound between the rings, between the noise.
The same with snow, especially when it's new.

I love the snow, the way it wipes the street
clear for a little while, before the dogs,
before the plows make muddy hills of it,
before the road salt and the sidewalk salt
dissolve it into dirty lakes and streams.
For a second it is clean and blank and quiet.
It's a miracle, how muted it can be,

like all the sound's absorbed into itself.
I like to stand outside there, on the street,
without the traffic in the early morning
with a new snowfall blanketing the street,

only my breath like feathers in the cold.
That's when I talk to God—don't laugh at me—
and actually feel for sure he's listening.

This one time I was driving, New Year's Day.
I was driving to a friend's. The road was empty.
It was early, just me and the snow
on long, slow curves between two mountain peaks:
a whiteout—road and trees and sky all white,
snow falling like a bed sheet on the hood.
Then, around a bend, a shadow in the road.

I didn't slow down. It was just a shadow.
But then, too late, I saw it was a deer
that had been run down by another car.
I wound up skidding halfway off the road.
When I got out, the place was a cathedral
with giant walls of white, even the deer
seemed pristine, a perfect antlered buck,

except for the halo of frozen blood
around its head. Its eyes were filled with snow,
I felt sick, kind of queasy, and I thought
that I should do something for this deer
like drag him to the shoulder, but I just
left him in that paradise of snow.
Was it the blood that made it seem so holy?

You bleed when you get a tattoo, don't you?
Sometimes I think of getting one. Today,
I woke up after dreaming that I had one,
in brilliant colors on a white background,

a streak of purple written into white,
on the slope of my back, all across my back,
indelible against a field of white.

V

I met this girl in Freiberg after the run,
where someone had a car, and we piled in
for the Schwartzwald hairpin drive to Prague for Easter.
The fields were filled with Soviet concrete,
with rusted pylons and abandoned trains,
just drying out like carrion in the sun.
In one small town, I crapped into a hole
in the ground from which a board had been removed.
We stayed a couple days in a family flat
belonging to some Czech friends of the girl—
Greta?—who later let me in her sleeping bag.

But it was after, in her dorm, the others gone,
when we actually shared a bed. By now it's spring.
On the morning of the day that I was leaving,
we made love in the cold lattice of sunlight
that came in through her window. It was nice,
and I remember thinking that my girlfriend
couldn't care who I slept with. I was happy
that I had someone, that soon I'd be leaving.
I felt giddy. I felt wrung out and loved,
if only briefly. Though it wasn't love
I felt exactly—more like free of love.
I was glad when it was time to get away,
to Paris on the Night Line sleeper train.

An oubliette—a train inside a tunnel.

"Was not that nobly done?"

I saw her one more time back in New York—
Sasha—and then again, I guess about a year ago,
six or seven months before she died.
It was suicide. I should have told you that.
She seemed okay, you know? She seemed . . . the same.
We drank a fifth of Scotch out of the bottle.
I was so wasted out on Amsterdam,
feeling sick and walking toward the train,
with the cold coming on and early dusk.
Seems a long time ago.
"I 'gin to be aweary of the sun . . ."

Sunlight shone on her face inside her room:
Is the body ever holy except in memory?

I learned
that I was capable of anything.

IV

THIS IS MY PROOF

Inside a book
I've been meaning to
read forever, I
come across you

decades later
and find again
words you wrote
to calm me when

we were together:
your photo pressed
like an aspen leaf
I guess I missed.

The scribble across
the back, your name —
if more was meant,
it never came.

There were others
(there's someone now),
same as you.
And yet, somehow

among dust motes,
none of it matters:
a rush of breath
comes in then scatters.

THE RESIDENCY

I love my cabin and my writing table,
my bright lunch pail, the mudded path. Then drinks
begin, say, five-ish — Stoli or Black Label —
and keep on till we've worked out all the kinks

in our disheveled psyches. Back at home,
it's hard how people don't know I'm an artist.
I feel as pointless as a garden gnome.
They think I'm ordinary: *that's* the hardest!

Here, they understand the mess that's me,
and everything about this place confirms
what I've known deep down since the age of three:
I operate on slightly different terms

than businessmen and lawyers and the crowd
that trades and dickers, hires and fires, and when
I tell the world my tale I tell it loud!
I must get down to breakfast before ten.

The cook, with every egg he scrambles, knows
that he is giving me fresh fuel to fashion
new Himalayas, draped in dazzling snows,
of imagination backed by skies of passion.

HIGH TO LOW

It's cringe-worthy yet also pleasing
when our host at lunch—someone I don't know
and whom I'm only meeting the first time—
sends back a bottle of expensive wine,
for no real reason. It's not just to show
his seasoned taste, a hard-won cultivation
              taken shape
over a lifetime studiously teasing
        savors from the grape.

A total creep, in fact, this guy,
a boor—he clearly doesn't give a rat's
who gets burned. (The waiter seems amused,
since after all these years he's gotten used
to jerks like this, and every bottle that's
returned he sips in secret at the back station.)
        This guy won't stand
for it: when life offends his nose or eye,
        he takes the upper hand.

His victories are mostly Pyrrhic,
but so what? Sure, he's obtuse but not blind
to the ways his huffy, prima donna poise
is oddly winning, even as it annoys.
Decorum is a thankless double bind,
a game for schmucks, an over-complication.
        Who ever bothers,
when no one cares for him (so goes the lyric),
        caring about others?

And would it make a difference
if he did? Not terribly. So, after lunch

he strolls down 43rd Street to Times Square.
A crane shot pulls back till he's barely there
amid the horn blasts and the traffic crunch,
a worker ant lost in an anthill nation.
                    And from a window
ten stories up, another man makes sense
          of this constant to-and-fro.

          In his lofty, godlike view,
the city assumes a manageable scope.
The air conditioning hums. Pressed to the glass,
his forehead feels the cool as people pass
beneath him, each one with a private hope
of getting his, by market calculation
                    or avid reach.
He, too, will do whatever he must do,
          each self for each.

          Pull back again and there is me
and you, watching this guy as his eyes light
on the man just come from lunch. His mild disdain
for something—jacket, shoes—is what remains,
after he casually blinks him out of sight.
And who, by further ghostly iteration,
                    takes stock of
us, is gauging us, and can they see
          us only from above?

CANCER DOG

Her open wound accuses you. It leaves
its traces in the corner where she sleeps.

She sleeps a lot and rises painfully.
Outside she sniffs at markings. It is spring.

Her limp complains you've already begun
to go, that you have gone with the betrayers.

Always in her view you are the arm
that, tied to her, is endlessly receding;

now there is no leader there to bind you
together, frayed apart or else gnawed through.

SCHNAUZER

Sit. You're making too much noise.
                              Bad boy.
Think about it: what's it going to look like,
you in my room, in just your underwear,
on an all-girls' floor in the freshman dorm?
I think you'd want to think about that fact.
I'll take that gag off, if you can sit still.
Okay, it's up to you. You know those cuffs
would hurt a lot less if you'd just relax.
Remember, you're the one who put them on.
You put them on. And then you just passed out,
like you were dead. I tried waking you, even
pried your lids up but your eyes were white,
which scared me 'cause I thought you might be dead.
I've never seen a person so . . . zoned out.
Sometimes, I try to imagine that *I'm* dead,
as if I weren't here, as if I was
invisible and I could walk around
with everything still going on without me.
What difference would it make if I were gone?
Like zero difference, you know what I mean?
It's okay with me. It's true. But nice of you
to try to disagree.
                     You're a sweetie.

I'm always blown away by people's kindness;
no, really, it just always knocks me out,
when someone drops the edginess we use
to keep away invaders, and, let's face it,
they're everywhere you go—the crosstown bus,
the grocery store, joggers in Central Park,
especially them, so smug, so master-race.

That's why I can't believe we ever met.
Not you and me. I mean this guy I loved.
I didn't really plan it, didn't ask for it,
you know, and that's how come I knew I loved him.
That's how it comes to you, not when you're looking,
but when your head is turned the other way.
I loved him. And I also loved his dog.
My dog loved *his* dog. That's the way we met,
at the dog run.

Actually, there were two near me:
a bigger run — much fancier but farther —
and, underneath the bridge, the scrappy one.
I started at the nicer one, you know,
walked down the extra blocks, because I thought,
since there were more dogs there, the better chance
of finding one that Lulu'd want to play with.
The nicer one had lots of dogs and space,
with little islands made of piled-up rocks.
But it was crap. The dogs there all were dead.
I mean they just seemed kind of dazed, like robots,
as if the life had just drained out of them —
like zombie dogs, *Night of the Living Dogs* —
or maybe they were all on Ritalin,
you know, the way they give that now to kids?
Meanwhile, the people there — the regulars —
they didn't notice. All they did was gossip,
blah-blah-blah, blah-blah, blah-blah, blah-blah,
talking about the way the neighborhood
had gone to hell and how they'd grown up there,
about their fancy breeders. Yak-yak-yak.
The dogs were sweet. Mostly they just looked stunned.

No one played with them or threw a ball.
People got annoyed when dogs would play,
but why else are they there—to rub and chase
and roll and hump each other in the dirt?
Lulu they just hated; she loved to run.
She'd tried to get the other dogs to chase her
by nipping at them; no, it wasn't biting.
Nipping. You'd put your finger in her mouth,
and she'd just hold it there between her teeth,
possess it, so you couldn't take it back,
but never hurting you, never, you see?
(Just grunt to let me know that you can hear me.)
But to them she was a wolf: blood-thirsty, feral,
and everyone would whisper when she came.

Then Lulu got a pigeon.
It wasn't her fault. I was standing right outside
the metal gate, where everyone could see us.
Lulu was a huntress; she hunted everything,
mice and squirrels, and earthworms she'd dig up.
But what she wanted most of all were pigeons.
Like those cartoons: the one's in which the dog's
pupils turn to drumsticks. She would pounce
at them, completely driven, every muscle
in her body, every hair on fire to catch
that bird, and not just catch it, eat it, too.
I've never seen her looking happier
than in that moment, when her choke collar
zipped tight like a big fish taking a hook,
and her leaping at it, airborne, twisting around
to catch it in her teeth.
The people freaked.

I started screaming, pulling on the leash,
but she had it in her mouth, between her paws.
When I reached in to free the thing, she growled,
and I came up with bloody hands and wrists.
It wasn't mine. Though I wondered if it was,
if she'd bitten me. But she would never do that.
Not even in the ecstasy of it.
That's another way that dogs are different.
They're hugely civilized, more so than we are.
So, that was it for the fancy uptown run.
We wound up at the dingy run in winter,
where the wind rips off the river, mostly empty,
where Lulu met Reynaldo, a scruffy schnauzer.
They ran until their tongues flapped down their chins.
Then Rey-Rey's owner started making small talk—
just casual, like stories from the paper,
training tricks, dog stories—like you do.

I waited on the days he didn't come.
It felt first like a little irritation,
so that I didn't notice it. But then
I actually ached for him when he was gone.
I told myself that Lulu missed Reynaldo,
but then one morning in the freezing rain
I saw him as we were coming along the river
towards the run, and Lulu started pulling
on her choke chain—she nearly pulled my arm off.
For two whole blocks she strained, just acting nuts.
She pulled the leash free of my hand and ran.
And as I stood there in the sleet I knew
that I had missed him so incredibly
I almost started crying. And the dogs,

leapt up to catch each other in their paws,
like ballroom dancers circling the floor,
upright, on hind legs, balanced arm in arm.
I felt like that was us, but not imagined it,
actually felt—as we stood there silently,
unmoving, watching, side-by-side—
that we were pressing up against each other,
swaying into the matted whorls of fur,
my teeth clamped on his skin, saliva flying.
I think I came. My legs let go a little.

I'm going to take these off, but understand
that once you leave this room you won't say anything.
Unless you want your father and the cops
to see these pictures on the Internet:
you look asleep, it's true, but how to explain it?
Sometimes I wonder if it isn't possible
that loves we have in our minds are the real ones,
the ones that matter to us most of all,
the ones that we take with us to the grave.
I guess I'm sorry that it won't be you
I'm supposed to love.
                    Now let me free your mouth.

BED OF ROSES

"Life's no bed of roses" is what they say.
Okay, well, fair enough.
We all know life is tough
(no one I can think of would deny it),
a senseless mayhem banked by mindless quiet.
Brutish, short. And yet we stay

and want to even when our time is up—
especially then, in fact,
our lives a muddy cataract
of taste and touch and sentimental feeling
draining away like shadows from the ceiling,
as we fish pills from a paper cup,

in a semi-private room—our last, we're told.
So no, no bed of roses.
But before the door closes
for good, it's worth remembering you do
know more or less that missing sense. Me, too.
I can easily pinpoint odd

moments when my own skin brushed against
the thornless side of life:
diving like a whetted knife
into the sapphire waters of the Med,
or lying naked, hip to hip, on a bed
of eelgrass discreetly dense.

Wasn't that a bed of roses, then?
The exact thing,
or just about. And doesn't a string
of those bright souvenirs make up our past,

gathered like beams of late sunshine casting
a glow on billowed curtains?

In a very real sense, they're all we've got,
these scatterings of love.
How strange that life should prove
a very bed of roses in the end
and nothing more, strewings of blessings, the kind
we mostly lived for and forgot.

A STOP BEFORE STARTING

The only time I've been to Switzerland
was early one spring on a train through the mountains.
There was a lake—I guess it was Lucerne?
Above me cliff tops ridged with snow fanned out
so that where I stood at the edge of the platform
light bathed the empty siding all around
with a diffused opalescence off the water.

Behind the station must have been a town,
spires of churches, municipal arcades,
and coffee squelching in the fogged cafés.
I never saw the place, though I remember
thinking *this* is Switzerland and took
a mind-shot of the pines, breathing-in the cold
as the porter whistled at us to reboard.

ARGUMENT FROM DESIGN

What of the watchmaker can we know from the watch?
That he was a careless sort, for one thing,
losing a perfectly good timepiece in high grass,
or that he made it for someone equally
careless, all his clockwork wasted.

Don't try to wind it now. Its springs,
like dried bird bones, have lost their springiness.
The tiny teeth of its gears are rotted out.
And from the age of the watch,
the watchmaker, too, must be similarly deteriorated.

So, in fact, there is a great deal of correspondence
between the maker and the thing he made.
That's pretty surprising, since
it seems almost never to work that way.
A radiant abstract painting, for example,
tells us nothing of the sad end of the artist
or what put those dark ideas in his head.

Or maybe that's all we do see
when we look at those paintings
or at a postcard of one
tacked above the desk on a cool summer night.

The causes don't stay causeless long
and, in hindsight anyway, make sense, we like to believe,
speeding on even after the watch has stopped.

BECALMED

for Rachel Wetzsteon

is anything but calm. Relict of wind, you are left to
the waves' whims. A thousand hammer strokes wear
at the spars, until an indolent rocking works slack
canvas free. You have for weeks foreseen a mangrove
harbor, though fearing the worst — that storms would
rob you of the dreamed chance to breathe again the
pine-dank hills of home. You had it precisely plot-
ted, despite the risk. Now the wind is out, and all
the tools of reckoning fall senseless. The teacups of
the anemometer dip this way and that and come up
dry. At night in your dark bunk, you hunker down
and pray that tomorrow morning brings the slightest
stirring, a ripple on the feckless swells. A great force
can whip a hurricane to land. A greater one sits like
an anvil on the sea's bruised surface until the zephyr
fails. She exhales then goes calm.

THE LANDING

Light goes pink on
the hulls of working boats
and on the boulders cropping out
from green islands opposite.
What's pent and riled

slackens, as ripples
lead our eyes along the passage.
The most difficult part is over,
the hardest is now past.
Twin vapor trails

criss-cross under
Scorpio. When a horse
shakes off its traces, it begins
to forget the lash, takes
shade and pungent hay.

What a fine day
it has become. From
the landing, I see the breeze
feathering the inlet. Such
excellent timing.

And you have come,
too, as I thought you might,
wordless at the water's edge.
And whether or not we
wind up like this

in time — as likely
it will be some antiseptic bed
or hairpin turn banded by ice —
my hope is this: just then,
I'll meet you here.

SOME PREVIOUS TITLES IN THE CARNEGIE MELLON POETRY SERIES

2013

Oregon, Henry Carlile
Selvage, Donna Johnson
At the Autopsy of Vaslav Nijinsky, Bridget Lowe
Silvertone, Dzvinia Orlowsky
Fibonacci Batman: New & Selected Poems, Maureen Seaton
When We Were Cherished, Eve Shelnutt
The Fortunate Era, Arthur Smith
Birds of the Air, David Yezzi

2012

Now Make an Altar, Amy Beeder
Still Some Cake, James Cummins
Comet Scar, James Harms
Early Creatures, Native Gods, K. A. Hays
That Was Oasis, Michael McFee
Blue Rust, Joseph Millar
Spitshine, Anne Marie Rooney
Civil Twilight, Margot Schilpp

2011

Having a Little Talk with Capital P Poetry, Jim Daniels
Oz, Nancy Eimers
Working in Flour, Jeff Friedman
Scorpio Rising: Selected Poems, Richard Katrovas
The Politics, Benjamin Paloff
Copperhead, Rachel Richardson

2010

The Diminishing House, Nicky Beer
A World Remembered, T. Alan Broughton

Say Sand, Daniel Coudriet
Knock Knock, Heather Hartley
In the Land We Imagined Ourselves, Jonathan Johnson
Selected Early Poems: 1958-1983, Greg Kuzma
The Other Life: Selected Poems, Herbert Scott
Admission, Jerry Williams

2009

Divine Margins, Peter Cooley
Cultural Studies, Kevin A. González
Dear Apocalypse, K. A. Hays
Warhol-o-rama, Peter Oresick
Cave of the Yellow Volkswagen, Maureen Seaton
Group Portrait from Hell, David Schloss
Birdwatching in Wartime, Jeffrey Thomson

2008

The Grace of Necessity, Samuel Green
After West, James Harms
Anticipate the Coming Reservoir, John Hoppenthaler
Convertible Night, Flurry of Stones, Dzvinia Orlowsky
Parable Hunter, Ricardo Pau-Llosa
The Book of Sleep, Eleanor Stanford

2007

Trick Pear, Suzanne Cleary
So I Will Till the Ground, Gregory Djanikian
Black Threads, Jeff Friedman
Drift and Pulse, Kathleen Halme
The Playhouse Near Dark, Elizabeth Holmes
On the Vanishing of Large Creatures, Susan Hutton
One Season Behind, Sarah Rosenblatt
Indeed I Was Pleased with the World, Mary Ruefle
The Situation, John Skoyles

2006

Burn the Field, Amy Beeder
The Sadness of Others, Hayan Charara
A Grammar to Waking, Nancy Eimers
Dog Star Delicatessen: New and Selected Poems, Mekeel McBride
Shinemaster, Michael McFee
Eastern Mountain Time, Joyce Peseroff
Dragging the Lake, Robert Thomas

2005

Things I Can't Tell You, Michael Dennis Browne
Bent to the Earth, Blas Manuel De Luna
Blindsight, Carol Hamilton
Fallen from a Chariot, Kevin Prufer
Needlegrass, Dennis Sampson
Laws of My Nature, Margot Schilpp
Sleeping Woman, Herbert Scott
Renovation, Jeffrey Thomson

2004

The Women Who Loved Elvis All Their Lives, Fleda Brown
The Chronic Liar Buys a Canary, Elizabeth Edwards
Freeways and Aqueducts, James Harms
Prague Winter, Richard Katrovas
Trains in Winter, Jay Meek
Tristimania, Mary Ruefle
Venus Examines Her Breast, Maureen Seaton
Various Orbits, Thom Ward

2003

Trouble, Mary Baine Campbell
A Place Made of Starlight, Peter Cooley
Taking Down the Angel, Jeff Friedman
Lives of Water, John Hoppenthaler
Imitation of Life, Allison Joseph
Except for One Obscene Brushstroke, Dzvinia Orlowsky